W9-BFC-670

Native
American
Peoples

SHOSHONE

Mary Stout

Gareth Stevens Publishing
A WORLD ALMANAC EDUCATION GROUP COMPANY

Please visit our web site at: **www.garethstevens.com**
For a free color catalog describing Gareth Stevens Publishing's list of high-quality books
and multimedia programs, call 1-800-542-2595 (USA) or 1-800-387-3178 (Canada).
Gareth Stevens Publishing's fax: (414) 332-3567.

Library of Congress Cataloging-in-Publication Data

Stout, Mary, 1954-
    Shoshone / by Mary Stout.
        p. cm. — (Native American peoples)
    Includes bibliographical references and index.
    ISBN 0-8368-4221-9 (lib. bdg.)
    1. Shoshoni Indians—History—Juvenile literature. 2. Shoshoni Indians—
Social life and customs—Juvenile literature. I. Title. II. Series.
E99.S4S77   2004
978'.0049745—dc22   2004046692

First published in 2005 by
Gareth Stevens Publishing
A World Almanac Education Group Company
330 West Olive Street, Suite 100
Milwaukee, WI 53212 USA

Copyright © 2005 by Gareth Stevens Publishing.

Produced by Discovery Books
Project editor: Valerie J. Weber
Designer and page production: Sabine Beaupré
Photo researcher: Tom Humphrey
Native American consultant: Robert J. Conley, M.A., Former Director of Native American
    Studies at Morningside College and Montana State University
Maps: Stefan Chabluk
Gareth Stevens editorial direction: Mark Sachner
Gareth Stevens art direction: Tammy West
Gareth Stevens production: Jessica Morris

Photo credits: Native Stock: cover, pp. 5, 8 (both), 11, 14, 17, 18, 19, 20 (both), 22, 24, 27
(bottom); Corbis: pp. 4, 7, 13, 21; Peter Newark's American Pictures: pp. 9, 12; AP/Wide World
Photos: pp. 10, 26, 27 (top); North Wind Picture Archives: p. 16; University of Nevada: p. 25.

Printed in the United States of America

1 2 3 4 5 6 7 8 9 09 08 07 06 05 04

Cover caption: This young Shoshone woman, Randy'l Teton, was the model for the new
Sacagawea golden dollar coin, issued in 2000.

Contents

Words that appear in the glossary are printed in **boldface** type the first time they appear in the text.

Origins

A Western Shoshone woman rests next to her grass-covered home as she weaves a traditional grass basket. Shoshone grass baskets are woven so tightly that they can hold water when sealed with tree resin.

The Land of the Shoshones

Wandering their traditional homelands of the Great Basin and high plains of the western United States in today's Nevada, Utah, Idaho, California, Montana, Oregon, and Wyoming, many Shoshone bands shared a language but not a lifestyle. The Shoshones called themselves *Nimi*, *Newe*, or *Nomo*, which means "the people." Over time, some bands **migrated** north and east and changed their lifestyles to suit the lands where they lived.

Today, more than 9,250 Shoshones (or Shoshonis) live on **reservations, colonies**, and *rancherias* in those states and across the United States. In Wyoming, the Eastern Shoshones share the Wind River Indian Reservation with the Arapahos. Most Northern Shoshones, who share a **culture** with the Bannocks, live on the Fort Hall Reservation in eastern Idaho. The Western Shoshones live on the Duck Valley Reservation in Nevada and in other Shoshone communities in Nevada, Utah, and California.

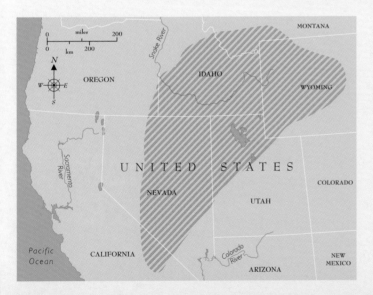

The traditional area wandered by the Shoshones included seven different states and many different landscapes — deserts, mountains, and plains.

These pictographs in Big Springs, Idaho, represent the Shoshones' origin story. Wolf and Coyote, who were brothers, were responsible for making the world the way it is.

Shoshone Origins

No one knows for sure where the Native Americans who settled in North America came from. Some scientists say that the **ancestors** of the Shoshones may have been from Asia and could have walked to North America over a landmass that may have once crossed the Bering Strait to Alaska during the last Ice Age.

Some Shoshones explain their origins differently. According to their traditional story, Wolf formed the earth from a mud ball, and Coyote filled the earth with people. His sons and daughters jumped out of a woven willow water jug Coyote carried across the land, which is why there are so many different Shoshone bands scattered over a large area.

Shoshone Language

Nearly twenty-three hundred people in the United States speak Shoshone. Here are a few words in their language.

Shoshone	Pronunciation	English
agai	ah-geh	salmon
baa	bah	rain
basigoo	bah-see-goh	camas root
bozhena	boh-jee-nah	buffalo
bungu	boon-goo	horse
deheya	duh-huh-yah	deer
gotoo	goh-toh	fire
izhape	ee-jah-puh	coyote

History

Western Shoshone History

Horseless, the Shoshones walked everywhere, using the abundant grasses growing on their lands for shelter and for food, which they produced from the seeds. They also gathered other foods as they found them. Their lifestyle remained largely unchanged until white miners discovered gold at the Comstock Lode in Nevada in 1857. This brought hordes of European-American settlers and miners to the area, who pushed out the Native Americans. The Shoshones fought back.

Shoshone raids on the settlers resulted in the 1863 **Treaty** of Ruby Valley, in which the Western Shoshones agreed to leave the settlers alone and live on a reservation in Ruby Valley in today's Nevada. Since the U.S. government did not provide that reservation, the Shoshones continued to live in communities in their traditional areas. In 1877, the government ordered all the Western Shoshones to move to the Duck Valley Reservation created for them on the Idaho-Nevada border. Some moved, but many Shoshones, unhappy with this solution, refused to go.

No More Living off the Land

As the settlers and their livestock overran Western Shoshone land, they ate or trampled sources of traditional Shoshone foods. Starving Shoshone men began working as cowboys on local ranches for wages, while the women became servants in the ranch houses.

In the early 1900s, the U.S. government realized that most Western Shoshones didn't live on a reservation and created colonies at Battle Mountain, Elko, and Duckwater in Nevada. Most of the California Shoshones moved up to the Owens Valley to share rancherias with the Paiutes, another Native tribe. Colonies were

California's Owens Valley, with Mount Whitney in the background, is home to many Western Shoshones, who moved there once their traditional territories could no longer support them.

small parcels of land given to the Native American tribes in Nevada. Too small to qualify as reservations, they were known as rancherias in California. By the late twentieth century, the Western Shoshones had only one full-size reservation at Duck Valley. Two-thirds of the Western Shoshones still live in tiny colonies, rancherias, or off-reservation near their traditional lands.

Gosiute Shoshones

Also called Goshutes, the Gosiute Shoshones are a branch of the Western Shoshones. They have been confused with the Utes and Paiutes, which explains the spelling of their name. The Gosiutes had the simplest lifestyle of all the Shoshones; they gathered pine nuts and seeds and lived in caves or piled up brush as a shelter. They wore little clothing, just **breechcloths** or aprons and moccasins, with rabbit-skin capes.

The Gosiutes attacked western stagecoaches, mail carriers, and settlers. In 1863, however, they signed the Tuilla Valley Treaty and now have two small reservations in their traditional territory at Deep Creek and Skull Valley, Utah.

Borrowing the idea from their Great Plains neighbors, the Northern Shoshones used tepees as their dwellings. Their sweathouses — small huts woven of willow branches, sagebrush, and/or grass — were still built the old way.

Northern Shoshone History

With similar cultures, Northern Shoshones and Bannocks lived in small bands in Idaho, south of the Salmon River, in the Columbia River plateau. In 1804, one member of the Lemhi band of Northern Shoshones was the first Northern Shoshone to see white explorers. Her name was Sacagawea, and she traveled with Meriwether Lewis and William Clark on their explorations across the western United States.

On August 17, 1805, explorers Meriwether Lewis and William Clark met a band of Shoshones led by the brother of their guide, Sacagawea. On their way to hunt buffalo, the Shoshones welcomed the explorers and traded some horses needed by the expedition. They camped together in Clark Canyon Reservoir, Montana (below), which Lewis named "Camp Fortunate."

On foot until other Native tribes traded horses with them in about 1700, the Northern Shoshones combined the Western Shoshone gathering society with the Eastern Shoshone's buffalo-hunting society. Unfortunately, the Blackfeet Indians, who already had horses and guns, began to take over Shoshone territory.

By 1850, settlers moving to Oregon crossed Northern Shoshone country in great numbers, and by 1860, the Mormons, a religious group, had settled in their territory. The Shoshones occasionally battled these intruders, fighting in the Bannock War of 1878 and the Sheepeater War of 1878 to 1879.

The Mormons moved westward to escape religious prejudice and settled in Utah, with the Utes and Shoshones as their only neighbors. Unfortunately, their cattle ate the same grasses that the Shoshones depended upon for survival, and they scared away the small game that the Shoshones hunted.

Tribal Lands Shrink

The U.S. government made several treaties with the Shoshones during the 1860s, establishing the 1,800,000-acre (730,000-hectare) Fort Hall Reservation in 1867 for the Northern Shoshones. The reservation did not remain this size for long, however. Settlers soon illegally moved to reservation land, and the growing town of Pocatello nearby required even more territory. Tribal lands shrank further when the Dawes Severalty Act of 1887 divided

These Shoshone-Bannock cowboys worked hard to move their cattle swiftly to stay ahead of a prairie fire during their annual roundup at their Fort Hall Reservation in 1958.

them and gave individual pieces to Native American families from 1911 through 1916. The lands were dry; many farms failed and were sold to non-Natives, again reducing the tribe's land holdings. By the 1950s, the Fort Hall Reservation covered only 524,000 acres (212,000 ha).

The Shoshones and Bannocks of Fort Hall organized as a tribe with a **constitution** in 1936. In 1963, the Indian Claims Commission awarded $8,864,000 to the Shoshone-Bannocks as a result of a 1946 Indian Claims Commission case against the

Bear River Massacre

The Northwestern Shoshones, a band of the Northern Shoshones, for the most part lived peacefully with their Mormon neighbors. Some men from another band of Shoshones stole a few cattle and horses from the settlers, who then asked for soldiers to protect them. On January 29, 1863, two hundred soldiers from the Third California Infantry Volunteers, led by Colonel Patrick Edward Connor, attacked the Northwestern Shoshone winter camp on the Bear River in Utah. The few weapons owned by the Shoshones were no match for the army's rifles. After four hours of fighting, at least 250 Shoshone men, women, and children lay dead, including Bear Hunter, the band's chief. This was the worst massacre of Native Americans in U.S. history, but few people know about it. A national historic landmark was finally put up at the Bear River massacre site in 1990.

government for the loss of their land. Two-thirds of the money was split among the tribal members and one-third given to the tribe as a whole. Their **economy** during the twentieth century has been based on farming, raising sheep and cattle, and **phosphate** mining.

Eastern Shoshone History

The Eastern Shoshone bands traditionally occupied an area in western Wyoming. Their hunting and gathering lifestyle was strongly affected by the Plains Indian horse culture. A highly organized, buffalo-hunting people, the Eastern Shoshones raided surrounding areas and hunted from horseback after getting horses in trade about 1700. From 1780 to 1825, constant warfare with the Blackfeet forced them farther west and reduced their numbers. Some Eastern Shoshones moved south and became known as the Comanches. Smallpox, a deadly disease, spread, killing many Shoshones and further weakening their society.

The Eastern Shoshones participated in an annual event during the 1820s through 1840 called the Green River Rendezvous. Native Americans, fur trappers, and traders gathered each summer near present-day Pinedale, Wyoming, to trade furs for goods, meet friends, and share news as shown in this 1870s painting. The rendezvous is still held each year during July.

Chief Washakie

Born in about 1804, Chief Washakie, a skilled warrior and powerful leader, helped both the Eastern Shoshones and the Americans. In 1850, Washakie became chief and sent warriors to help the Americans moving west. He also allowed the railroad builders to safely lay tracks through Shoshone country. As scouts for the U.S. Army, Washakie and his warriors helped fight other enemy Native American tribes.

The U.S. government, however, did not fulfill its promises to Washakie and the Shoshones. Though it gave the Eastern Shoshones the Wind River Valley Reservation, it did not provide the schools, seeds, tools, and livestock as promised in the Fort Bridger Treaty. When he died in 1900, Washakie was buried with full U.S. military honors at Fort Washakie.

After a legendary one-on-one battle with a Crow chief over control of the Wind River Valley, Chief Washakie emerged as victor.

Chief Washakie rose to power from 1825 to 1880 and restored the spirit and strength of the Eastern Shoshones. Avoiding conflict with the U.S. government, he worked with it on the first Fort Bridger Treaty of July 3, 1863, to establish the Shoshone Reservation, which originally included more than 44 million acres (18 million ha) in Colorado, Utah, Idaho, and Wyoming. Further agreements and treaties shrunk the Shoshone Reservation, and in 1878, the U.S. government sent the Shoshones' old enemies, the Arapahos, to share the reservation with them and later renamed it the Wind River Reservation. Today, the Wind River Reservation, home to both the Eastern Shoshones and Arapahoes, covers 2,268,000 acres (918,000 ha).

> Before the [settlers] passed through my country, buffalo, elk, and antelope could be seen. . . . Now, when I look for game, I see only wagons with white tops and men riding upon their horses.
>
> *Chief Washakie, 1858*

The Eastern Shoshones Recover

During the twentieth century, most of the Eastern Shoshones depended upon the U.S. government for food, jobs, and education. In 1939, the Shoshones successfully sued the government to have some of their tribal lands restored, and their reservation was enlarged to its present size. They received $3.5 million for economic development, and the tribal council took over governing the reservation from the U.S. government. Since 1945, the Shoshones experienced some population growth, new jobs, stability, and a growing Arapaho influence on the reservation, but progress has remained slow in the face of continuing social problems.

In 1988, the Eastern Shoshone **unemployment** rate at Wind River was 71 percent, and poverty was the main issue. Because of the poor Wyoming economy, young Shoshones began leaving the reservation for better education and employment.

Both Native American and white children attended the government school on the Wind River Reservation as shown in this 1939 photograph.

13

Traditional Way of Life

The Shoshone bands each developed their own unique customs but shared some practices in common.

Wrapped in soft hides, this Shoshone baby is protected in his traditional cradleboard.

Childhood

Shoshone childbirth customs were practical, such as asking a woman relative to help with the birth. To protect their skin from the sun, babies were covered with a paste made of clay. They were wrapped in skins and carried in **cradleboards** on their mothers' back. Young children spent time helping their parents look for and gather food or playing with household items. As they grew older, boys played in groups and hunted rabbits, birds, and other small animals, or they helped the older hunters. Older girls helped with household chores and cared for the younger children.

Adolescence

When Shoshone girls became teenagers, they were isolated in a hut for a few days while their mothers spoke with them about proper behavior. They were then considered ready for marriage. No customs existed for a boy's coming of age, except among the Eastern Shoshones, whose boys might go on a **vision quest**.

Marriage and Death

The Shoshone bride and groom or their families could arrange a marriage. In some cases, the groom kidnapped the bride and forced her to marry him. Men could have more than one wife, and women could have more than one husband. Often, a man would have to work for the bride's family before he could marry her. Both marriage and divorce were casual and without ceremony.

Death customs differed from band to band. At death, a Shoshone's body might be burned to ashes, buried in a cave, or placed in a rock crevice. The California Shoshones held a mourning ceremony one year after a person's death to sing, talk about the person, and destroy his or her belongings.

∼∼∼∼ Eastern Shoshone Vision Quest ∼∼∼∼

According to Eastern Shoshone traditions, a teenage boy could obtain **supernatural** powers in several ways. He could have dreams giving him power, or a medicine man might transfer his power to the boy. He might go on a vision quest by visiting one of his band's **sacred** places to pray and sleep alone in hopes of obtaining supernatural powers. If he was successful, he would see a **vision** of a *poha* (some aspect of nature, such as an animal, bird, sun, or wind) that showed him a small object such as a rock that contained power for him or gave him a song or protection.

Western Shoshone Traditional Life

The Western Shoshones relied upon plant gathering for food. From spring through fall, small family groups wandered over a large area gathering seeds, grasses, and plants. In a few weeks, a Shoshone family of four could gather 1,200 pounds (540 kilograms) of pine nuts, their most important food. They used woven grass baskets to store their seed harvest. The men and boys also hunted rabbits and other small animals.

During the winter, many families gathered together at a winter camp. Made from poles, brush, and bark, the Shoshones' winter home was cone-shaped. Women wore hats and skirts of grass, bark, or animal skins, and men wore skin breechcloths. Everyone put on rabbit-skin blankets and moccasins when it got cold.

Western Shoshones did not have permanent chiefs. When families gathered for a rabbit hunt or festival or in their winter village, the oldest able man was temporarily in charge.

Seeds of the pinion pine tree, pine nuts (also called pinion nuts or seeds) nestle inside a hard shell that must first be removed. The Shoshones ground these nuts to make a fine meal that they added to soups or used like flour in baking.

Festivals were for visiting, gambling, and dancing, especially the popular round dance, where many people danced in a circle, accompanied by a singer and drummer. Although the Western Shoshones had few religious ceremonies, men and women spoke directly to the spirits and could acquire a supernatural power through dreams and visions.

Recognized as works of art today, Shoshone woven grass baskets were used to store seed harvests.

Games

Games were very popular, and adult Western Shoshones liked to bet on their outcomes. In shinny, teams of women hit a small ball across a goal line with a stick. In the ball race, two teams of men kicked a stuffed animal-skin ball to the finish line. Two teams also played the bone game, a Shoshone favorite, where a member held a plain bone in one hand and one wrapped with leather or grass cord in the other. Teams had to guess which hand held the plain bone.

Northern Shoshone Traditional Life

Although the Northern Shoshones hunted buffalo in large groups like other Plains Indians, fish provided much of their food. Ranging along the Snake River, the Shoshones caught salmon, trout, perch, and other fish. They also collected camas lily and other roots to eat and hunted elk, deer, and sheep in the mountains.

The Northern Shoshones traded extensively, gaining horses and exchanging furs for other goods. Some Shoshone bands lived in tepees like their Plains neighbors, while others built small, cone-shaped lodges of woven willow branches covered with sage and grass.

The camas lily is a beautiful blue wildflower that grows on the Plains. The bulb at its root, shown here, was a favorite Shoshone food when cooked.

The Northern Shoshone bands usually had no chief, unless they were doing something where leadership was necessary, such as gathering for a ceremony, a buffalo hunt, or other community event. Anyone who was brave and a good leader could be a chief; chiefs often changed from event to event.

Their ceremonies were dances held to celebrate the salmon and ask for a good food supply. Like their Eastern Shoshone neighbors, the Northern Shoshones performed the Sun Dance ceremony to bring good to the tribe.

Chief Tendoy of the Lemhi band of Northern Shoshones arranged to have a small reservation set aside for his band in 1875 in the Lemhi Valley, their traditional area. In 1906, the reservation was closed down, and the Shoshones had to move to the Fort Hall Reservation. Chief Tendoy died in 1907.

~~~ Sun Dance Ceremony, A Solemn Ritual ~~~

A vision reveals to a chief that he must sponsor a Sun Dance ceremony, which includes several dances. He invites others to help him, and they erect a center pole with twelve smaller poles encircling it, acting as boundaries. In the dance area, singers and drummers sit in the southeast section, onlookers in the northeast section, and the dancers themselves occupy the rest of the area. People who have decided to become dancers will dance for three days without food or water. They are dancing for visions and power for themselves and for the health and well-being of their community.

Eastern Shoshone Traditional Life

Following the available food sources, the Eastern Shoshones roamed across today's Wyoming, settling in different places for months. In addition to buffalo, the men caught fish and hunted deer, sheep, and rabbits. The women gathered roots, seeds, berries, and spring shoots, cared for children, and created leather work, especially leather bags called parfleches. They lived in tepees made of tanned buffalo hides.

The Eastern Shoshones believed that all living things had spirits and sought supernatural powers from these spirits through prayers, dreaming, and vision quests. They also held group ceremonies, especially the Sun Dance and the Shuffling Dance, held at night during the winter when they sang sacred songs praying for the welfare of the tribe.

Among the Eastern Shoshones, women created leather work. They gained prestige and respect by making beautifully decorated parfleches, which were used by the family, given as gifts, and traded for other goods.

War and Trade

The Eastern Shoshones' leader was typically an important older military man respected by the tribe. His leadership determined the strength or weakness of the whole tribe. Because they were involved in the fur trade and were constantly at war

Shoshone women used the type of digging stick shown above (top) to pull up various plants and roots such as the camas lily bulbs. One method of catching fish involved using a woven fish trap, pictured above (bottom).

This vivid hide painting shows a buffalo dance after a hunt. The horse's tail has been tied up for war.

with other tribes, good hunters, traders, and warriors were important people in Eastern Shoshone society.

Both horses and dogs were necessary to the Shoshones for transportation, hunting, and war. If a horse was wounded in war, it would be painted and decorated with feathers in its mane and tail.

Yellow Brows

Named for the short, brushlike strip of hair that its members colored yellow, the Yellow Brows were one of two Eastern Shoshone military societies. To become a Yellow Brow, a young man had to prove himself in battle and go through a backward speech ritual, where everyone said the opposite of what was meant. It was the job of these brave, young warriors to protect and defend their tribe and to organize the large, tribal buffalo hunts. A group of 100 to 150, the Yellow Brows were the first to go into battle. Before fighting, the Yellow Brows and their horses danced the Big Horse Dance to prepare for battle.

Today

Contemporary Shoshones

Today, Shoshones may live on reservations, colonies, or rancherias or in numerous American communities. Their lifestyle is similar to that of other Americans, but they still maintain their tribal identities. Some Shoshone children attend tribal schools on the reservation; others go to local public schools. Since the 1960s, many Shoshone communities have renewed their tradition of annual festivals.

Begun in the 1990s, the Shoshone Tribal Cultural Center on the Wind River Reservation provides tribal history and teaching of the Shoshone language and traditional arts and crafts. Religion is still very important, and many Eastern Shoshones participate in the Sun Dance and in the Native American Church, which

In 1998, students from Shoshone-Bannock High School in Fort Hall, Idaho, were the first Native Americans to send a science experiment on a space shuttle. Their third experiment remained unfinished when the space shuttle *Columbia* crashed upon reentry in 2003.

combines Native beliefs and customs with Christianity. **Powwows**, introduced in 1957, have become important social and cultural events. In the 1970s, Shoshone women began to sing, drum, and perform some dances traditionally done by men. This has increased interest and participation in traditional ceremonies.

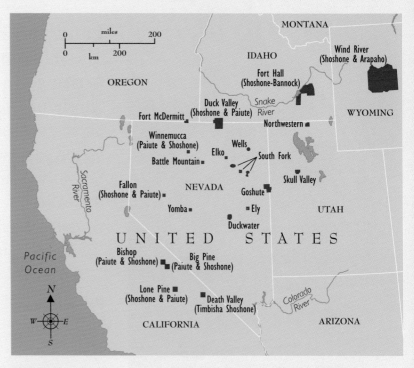

Shoshones today live on and off their reservations, colonies, and rancherias. The Western Shoshones are still fighting for their homeland.

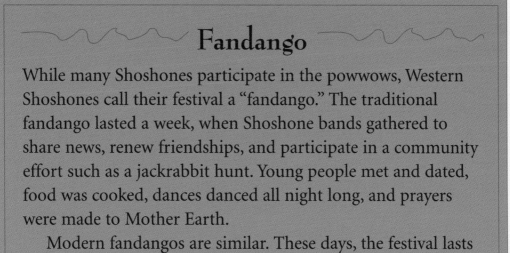

Fandango

While many Shoshones participate in the powwows, Western Shoshones call their festival a "fandango." The traditional fandango lasted a week, when Shoshone bands gathered to share news, renew friendships, and participate in a community effort such as a jackrabbit hunt. Young people met and dated, food was cooked, dances danced all night long, and prayers were made to Mother Earth.

Modern fandangos are similar. These days, the festival lasts Friday through Sunday and includes a barbecue, games, traditional songs and dances, and arts and crafts.

Land and Economy

The Shoshone land base continues to change. In 2000, the Timbisha Shoshones, part of the Western Shoshones, began a new reservation in Death Valley, California. Since there are no jobs or housing there, no one lives on the Northwestern Shoshone band's 184 acres (75 ha) in Utah.

Government improvement programs rarely help those Western Shoshones not living on large reservations. In 1948, the U.S. government established the Nevada Test Site in Western Shoshone traditional territory to test nuclear bombs and other weapons and forced about one hundred families to move. **Radiation** from these tests might be responsible for a high Shoshone cancer rate today.

While modern powwows feature food, friendship, and Native American traditional arts, attention often focuses on the dance competition. Here, a Shoshone girl performs a shawl dance.

The Northern Shoshones on the Fort Hall Reservation established a **casino** in 1990 that brings in tourists. They also promote education in both English and Shoshone, publish a local newspaper called the *Sho-Ban News*, and hold an annual rodeo and festival each August.

The money gained from leasing the right to big businesses to drill for oil and gas on their land contributes to the tribal economy of the Eastern Shoshones, as does ranching and farming. The unemployment rate is still high, however, and young people leave the reservation for better education and employment opportunities.

Shoshone Arts and Literature

Many Shoshones contribute to American arts and literature, bringing their own unique ideas. Based upon the traditional craft of weaving baskets to store seed harvests, Shoshone grass basketry thrives as an art form today. Sandra Okuma, who is Shoshone-Bannock and Luiseno, paints pictures of Native Americans that focus on the detail and beauty of traditional or powwow clothing. Her daughter, Jamie, creates soft sculptures with elaborate beadwork. Both mother and daughter won awards at the Santa Fe Indian Market in 2000.

A Shoshone-Chippewa poet, nila northSun, writes about her Shoshone family in her poems; one poem tells about her grandmother being kidnapped by her husband to run away and get married. Her most recent book is called *A Snake in Her Mouth: Poems, 1974–96.*

Shoshone poet nila northSun, a former powwow princess, lives on the Fallon Paiute-Shoshone Reservation, where she is the director of Stepping Stones, a shelter for at-risk Native American teens.

Jack Malotte, Graphic Artist

A former teacher, carpenter, and cowboy, Western Shoshone Jack Malotte is a well-known graphic artist. He loves painting landscapes but is most famous for his humorous and political paintings. His pictures show what it's like to be a traditional Indian in a modern American world. The Smithsonian's National Museum of the American Indian featured his work in its "Indian Humor" exhibition.

New information in 2004 questions the safety of Yucca Mountain as a dumping place for nuclear waste. Western Shoshone tribal members have fought against the selection of Yucca Mountain for years, staging protest ceremonies such as this one.

Current Shoshone Issues

In 2002, the U.S. government selected Yucca Mountain, located 100 miles (160 km) northwest of Las Vegas, Nevada, to store the country's highly **radioactive** nuclear waste on a long-term basis. The Western Shoshones consider Yucca Mountain to be a sacred place and are fighting against this use of their traditional lands.

Since their casino opened, the Shoshone-Bannock Tribe (Northern Shoshone) has been in a legal battle with the Idaho government, which does not want any gambling or casinos within the state. Finally in 2000, the Idaho governor signed a law that would allow the tribe to have a casino, but disagreements continue over what types of machines will be allowed there.

In our traditional and cultural and spiritual ways, land is not a real estate. Life cannot exist without land. Everything that you and I wear comes from this land in one way or another, and it's important.... It's life...."

Carrie Dann, April 11, 2003

The most controversial issue faced by the Shoshones concerns the lack of land for the Western Shoshones. Because the Western Shoshones lost their homeland to American settlers, the Indian Claims Commission approved of paying them $26 million in 1979. These funds were never given to the tribe, partly because some Western Shoshones were afraid that if they accepted the money, they would never get their land back.

Carrie and Mary Dann

Two Western Shoshone grandmothers in their sixties and seventies have fought the U.S. government for over thirty years. Carrie and Mary Dann live on the same land where their family has always lived; their horses and cows roam the area. The U.S. government says that it owns the land, and the Danns should pay fees to keep their livestock there. It has charged the Danns over $3 million in fines. Carrie and Mary Dann refuse to pay, saying that the land is theirs.

The Dann sisters have been recognized many times and given international awards for their ongoing struggle with the U.S. government. They continue to live on their family ranch in Nevada.

In 2003, the U.S. Senate also approved paying the Western Shoshones their money, which now totals $142 million. The Western Shoshone National Council and others went to court in 2003, however, to ask for the return of 60 million acres (24 million ha) in four states, the original Shoshone homeland that they call *Newe Sogobia*.

An Ongoing Culture

Today's Shoshones face difficult modern issues such as poverty and unemployment. They are also fighting to maintain their traditional lands, keep their sacred places untouched, and educate people about their special history and culture. Keeping their traditional communities alive helps give them the strength to continue their struggles.

These Northern Shoshone girls have fun together at a local celebration. Pride in their heritage will help keep the Shoshone tribe strong.

Time Line

1804–06   Meriwether Lewis and William Clark explore the West; Sacagawea, a Lemhi Shoshone, helps guide the party.

1848   Gold rush begins in Nevada, bringing whites to Shoshone land; Shoshone country becomes part of the United States.

1857   Comstock Lode silver and gold rush in Nevada.

1863   Bear River Massacre in Utah results in hundreds dead; Western Shoshones in Nevada sign Ruby Valley Treaty; first Fort Bridger Treaty is signed with the Eastern Shoshones.

1867   Fort Hall Reservation established for Northern Shoshones in Idaho.

1868   Second Fort Bridger Treaty establishes the present-day Wind River Reservation for the Eastern Shoshones in Wyoming.

1877   Duck Valley Reservation established for some Western Shoshone bands on Nevada-Idaho border.

1878–79   Shoshones fight in Bannock War and Sheepeater War.

1887   Dawes Severalty Act divides tribal land into individual pieces, putting tribe at risk of losing land.

1893   Duck Valley Reservation boarding school is started.

1917   Colonies are created for some Nevada Shoshone bands.

1948   Nevada Test Site established on traditional Western Shoshone lands; government pushes Native Americans from land.

1963   Indian Claims Commission awards $15.7 million to all Shoshones for their loss of land.

1982   U.S. government recognizes Western Shoshones as a tribe and has to deal with them as a separate nation.

1990   Shoshone-Bannocks open a casino, bringing tourist dollars to tribal economy; Bear River Massacre site gets a historic marker.

2002   Yucca Mountain, Nevada, selected for nuclear-waste storage on traditional Western Shoshone lands.

2003   U.S. Senate approves the $142 million Indian Claims Commission award to the Western Shoshones for their loss of land.

Glossary

ancestors: people from whom an individual or group is descended.

breechcloths: strips of cloth worn around the hips.

casino: a building with slot machines and other gambling games.

colonies: small reservations given to Native Americans in Nevada.

constitution: the basic laws and principles of a nation that outline the powers of the government and the rights of the people.

cradleboards: portable cradles made of a board or frame onto which a baby is secured with blankets or bindings.

culture: the arts, beliefs, and customs that form a people's way of life.

economy: the way a country or people produces, divides up, and uses its goods and money.

migrated: moved from one place to another.

phosphate: a mineral that is used in fertilizers and strong cleansers.

powwows: celebrations of Indian culture, usually including singing, drumming, dancing, giving thanks, and connecting with loved ones.

radiation: any rays given off by a radioactive substance; they can change people's cell structure and, in high doses, often cause cancer.

radioactive: describes materials that are dangerous because they can change the cell structure of everything they come into contact with.

rancherias: small reservations given to Indians in California.

reservations: lands set aside by the government for tribes to live on.

sacred: having to do with religion or spirituality.

supernatural: beyond the natural world; something that cannot be seen, especially relating to gods and spirits.

treaty: an agreement among two or more nations.

unemployment: the number of people without jobs.

vision: something seen or experienced that is not from this world but the supernatural one; visions resemble dreams but the person is awake.

vision quest: an adventurous journey to seek spiritual power from the supernatural world.

More Resources

Web Sites:

http://www.easternshoshone.net Home page for the Eastern Shoshone Tribe and the Wind River Indian Reservation.

http://www.isu.edu/~loetchri Follow links on the Shoshoni Language Home Page to an English-Shoshoni dictionary and to learn to count in Shoshoni.

http://www.pbs.org/lewisandclark/inside/saca.html For information on Sacagawea, her life, and her valuable role as guide to the Lewis and Clark expedition to find the West Coast.

http://www.sho-ban.com/index.asp Describes the Fort Hall Indian Reservation and gives a brief history of the Shoshone and Bannock tribes.

http://thesierraweb.com/sightseeing/deathvalley/dvnative.html For information about the Timbisha Shoshone Reservation in Death Valley, California.

Books:

Alter, Judy. *Sacagawea: Native American Interpreter.* Child's World, 2003.

Bial, Raymond. *The Shoshone* (Lifeways). Benchmark Books, 2002.

Blackhawk, Ned. *The Shoshone* (Indian Nations). Raintree Steck-Vaughn, 2000.

Erdich, Liselotte. *Sacagawea.* Carolrhoda Books, 2003.

Keller, Kristen Thoennes. *The Shoshone: Pine Nut Harvesters of the Great Basin.* Blue Earth Books, 2003.

Mattern, Joanne. *The Shoshone People* (Native Peoples). Bridgestone Books, 2001.

Ryan, Marla Felkins. *Shoshone.* Blackbirch Marketing, 2003.

Things to Think About and Do

Imagine and Write

If you were a member of a band named for the main food that you liked to eat, what would be the name of your band? Write a paragraph describing your band's lifestyle and food-gathering activities, just as the Shoshones have been described. Share your band description with others, and discuss how you are different from and how you are the same as the Shoshones.

Hand Game

Get two sticks, about 3 inches (8 centimeters) long and as thick as your finger, that look alike. Wrap and tie a piece of yarn around one of the sticks. Place a cloth over your hands and pass the sticks from one hand to another. Stop, and have someone remove the cloth, and ask the watchers to guess which hand holds the plain stick.

Picture Writing

The Shoshones painted small pictures on leather to record their history. Pretend your writing uses pictures, not words. Paint a series of small pictures to tell about one event in Shoshone history.

Debate

Have a group of people break into two teams. One team answers "yes" to the following question, and one team answers "no" to the question: "Should the U.S. government give the Western Shoshones land for a large reservation?" Each team should give reasons for its answer.

Index